Omar Hamaoui aka Baby O

# SAVED BY THE PEN

First edition, Turning Point Books, 2024
www.tpbooksonline.com
turningpoint_books


Text editing by Tala Smiley


Illustrations by Tengiz Begoidze


Layout design by Gail Saab

Printing by 53 Dots

ISBN 978-9953-972-29-9

# TABLE OF CONTENTS

CHAPTER I

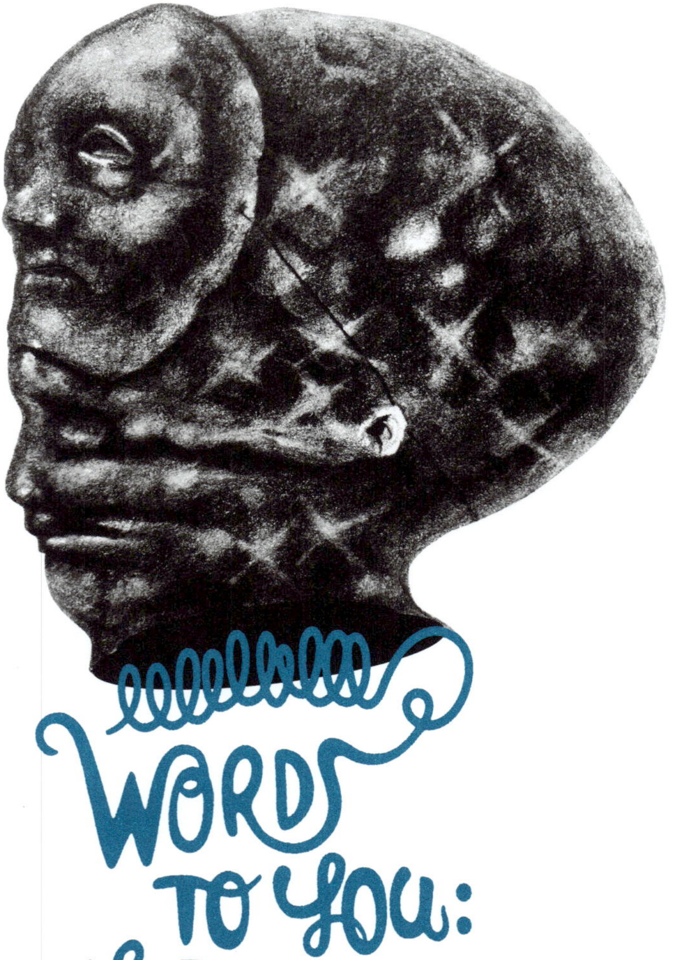

# WORDS TO YOU: LETTERS TO DAD

## 1.1. BECAUSE OF YOU, I CAN'T

With every fibre,

I attempt to divert
from the intrusive constant
that rattles between my ears.

Because of you,

I can't help but feel incomplete.

Keep you at an arm's length
to shield,

yet I'm yearning
to disarm
so that I don't cut you out.

The stitching of my soul
has your acceptance as the yarn.
But I don't have the tools to piece it together.

Because of you,

I've not known what it means to put myself first.
Grown into a forever teen that just knows
how to quench his thirst.
Chest burns,
after drowning in the residue
that dulls the sharp blade
in the shape of guilt.

What makes it worse?

I knowingly cut this pattern
that I embody to mask what's beneath,
into this rugged olive branch quilt
with lashings of ink,

broken up by battle wounds
of a conflict between the two
inhabiting the chipped boulders.

Because of you,

I had to sprout before spring,
leaving a mutilated unripe fruit

whilst a parasite drained what was left.

Growing was put on hold.

Am I partly to blame?
Who knows,
all that is clear.

Because of you,
because of me,

we weren't as harmonious
as we should have been.

## 1.2. WHEN AN ELEPHANT CLEARS A FOREST IT'S ONLY THEIR FOOTMARKS THAT ARE LEFT

To an industry, a pioneer.
To many, a leader.
To a family, a head.
To lots, a friend.
To a few, an idol.
To Alia, Marina, Mum, and I,
You were everything.
I've tried to put my emotions into words a few times since the loss of your life.
I sit here pen in hand, shaking, waiting to find the words.
How can I share what I've felt for someone who was my entire world?
Because you see, Issam Izzat Hamaoui
cannot be described with mere sentences
but, I've sentenced myself to try for you.
Calm as your baby blue eyes,
but a fire inside that could tear down every one of your lies.
A smile that wouldn't fit inside.
But a command that you wouldn't even try to deny.
Small in stature, yes.
Larger than life, always looking for the best.
A funny knack of making everyone feel welcome.
But we all knew the fact that you had to be the centre of attention.
A simple grasp and peck of one's hand you were ready to give all of your affection.
But a stern look and snap of your head, detention.
Everything you ever did was for what you held most precious.
Your presence, infectious.
A streak of rebelliousness.

Generosity, overzealous.

Your love, endless.

But never reckless.

When I heard the news it felt like a piece of my soul was ripped out from under me.

But maybe, just maybe, it's your presence trying to fit inside of me.

Filling the cracks that have been felt to last for my entirety.

You will live through me for eternity.

The image of you with beads in your hand.

Shuffling your feet like you were in sand.

Marching your band.

A rose you will always stand.

I battled with an emotion of a notion that you didn't know I loved you.

A struggle from a ripe age that I always knew I was going to lose you too soon.

Do I protect myself and not get too close or do I lose my everything?

Was a question I'd frequently ask myself.

Never did I think I'd reach peace.

But alas I think it's within me.

Issam.

A river of emotion.

Every fibre of you, devotion.

Promotion of everyone who stood by you.

When you spoke, it was almost in slow-motion.

Never any commotion.

All ears on your expressed notion.

Baba.

I love you as much as the ocean.

CHAPTER 2

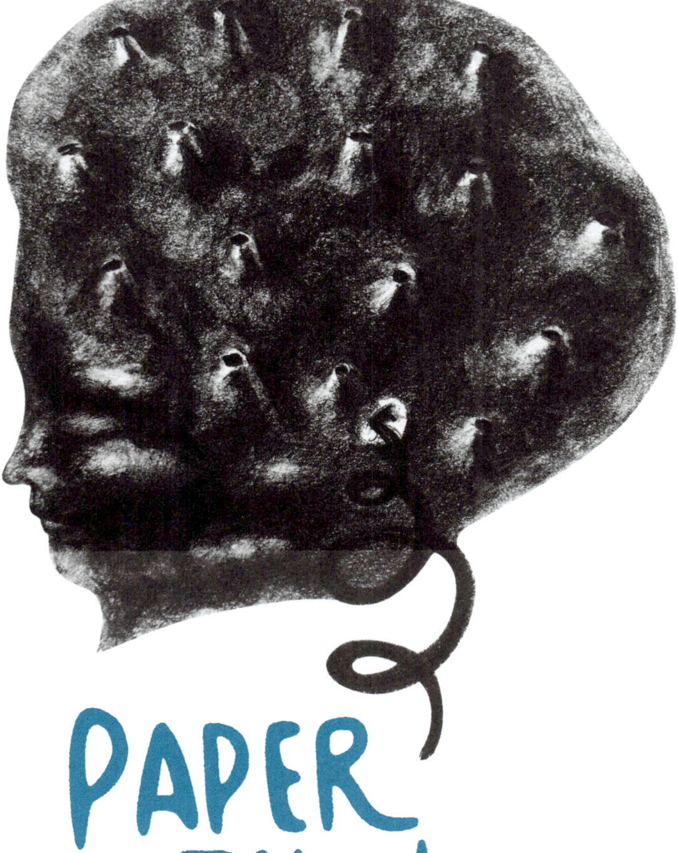

# PAPER THIN: WORDS OF STRUGGLE

## 2.1. BRANDED LIKE CATTLE

I've etched ink into my skin
to tell you a story so that I

don't have to.

Good things happen in

one
two
and three.

But hell's gates
open to the same beat.

After fleeing
from our century's plague,
compass to the birthplace of a painter
who touched paper with paint.

To lose oneself on the trek
towards the land of pink.
Boots of covid treason
journey people stuffed to the brink.

Arm-in-arm, like the ruling,
breaking the 10 feet.
Landed a group
who were just to meet.
-
As if the first two months picked
from a scene from Aciman.
Picnics in fields of strawberries,
bubbly laughter rising to the summit.

A sonnet of kissing behind open doors,
little songs of, "just one more".
Like the slow drumbeat of a leaking faucet,
each sun-kissed day set

to a setting of sitting under
a grandiose oak
where a marriage of cackling
masked the thunder of steel to plate.

Trinkets filled with our land's grape
never an eye to, "let's lay".

This is where
the devil comes to play.

With a brush of its horn.
Infested a tumor to the belly
of the gentle beast.
Her coat was the only
buffer when I chained
myself behind lock and key.

Lowered a sheet of myself
into her final resting bed.
Tied to the garden,
ashes to be spread.
-
Fluttering grey particles
dancing in unison with a silo,
rumbled a catastrophe
never to be seen.

A week passed, for a kick
to bring a nation to its knees,
a city's hoarse lungs
exploding with pneumonia

as it neighs with a trait
of a mushroom cloud
planted to bury home,
land under rubble.

Thousands displaced.
Millions of hearts trodden.
A humped haystack on the back,
surely that was the last straw?

Maybe this was my seductive lover,
the caped shadowed figure, K?
With her arm around my neck
keeping me hostage.

Taxing me for slipping the border
and enjoying the forbidden fruit of nature.
She knocks furiously
at the multiple storied barn door

arising through the hypnotic
columns of the South.
She tears through the wheat valleys,
akin to her kin, Hestia,
harvesting fragmented
shards of my soul.

I open to confront her,
to stand eye-to-eye.
She dealt her final blow,
played her final hand.
The rule of three
was complete.
-
On the clearest summer's day
floating on a cocktail
of clouded grievance
and the shaking blood of Jesus,
a storm came stampeding
without any haste.

Swept away the deepest blue
and took my father away.

A chapter closed;
his soul joined
his kin.

A mammoth of a man who withstood
conflict between the red line's trench,
Those who can't be named attempted settlement,
and eating from a park bench
but this was the nail in the coffin,
the camel's back was broken.

## 2.2. HORIZONTAL THOUGHTS

Thought it'd be great that I share my time of late,
sitting on the window, no food for dinner.

At this time, doubt fills me like the glass half empty,
can't sprout foundations, vacant,
days fly to night, isolation stays weighted.

Pick yourself up.
You've got so much.
You're doing so well.
Make the right choices.

Leave like the leaves,
can't branch out;
the pain is too great.

The term,
lie low,
might turn to forever though.

My spiritual flow is dying slow
beginning to look mucky,

can't decide whether it's the weather
or I've taken the wrong right,

axial tilt has got me thinking
about slitting the guilt.

## 2.3. UNHEROIC DECLARATION

Dragging my sorry carcass
from the East to West

I stretch and break my neck
to wake from rest.

I rattle fibs and sib[1] myself,
my heart pinned to nine-inch nails.

Time is no more
than a number of late
I lie in wait
to take what has forever seemed
to be my fate.

The constant berating
of neither joy
nor torment

has left me questioning

my sanity,

can I put an index on my existence?
Fluid interests seeping
down
my oesophagus.

Replies hit my cranium from a cavity,
questions left on the kitchen sink.
But no matter how big the latter,

Mr. Answer never shows what he thinks.



[1] Sib is an Arabic word that means 'swear'.

## 2.4. HOME NO LONGER EXISTS

Hallowed corridors intersect empty streets
Ominous stretches of stillness meet
Meaning of being, left at tiny beats
Ethereal feelings no more but an unreachable feat,

Nature's course questioned, questioned, questioned.
Oblivious to these life lessons, lessons, lessons.

Listening out for cantica of despair
Oh 'mare blared into the glistening nights glare,
No weight can we longer bare,
Guts to admit that what's needed is a fare out of here
Erect regret that we failed to keep our light flared,
Raging beings tamed by a mere prayer.

Engulfed in a need to develop a sense of being.
Xanax smiles from every ceiling, beaming.
I cannot but help accept that I've lost my meaning.
Scratch at the bloody skin to find what's within, peeling.
Talons deep, watch the bleeding.
Stuck, what a feeling.

## 2.5. CUT TO THE BONE

I peel my layers back,
relentlessly digging to the pit of my existence,
pulling deeper into the abyss.
Will anyone hear me while I keep the door ajar?
Unknowing if I'll be able to stay in this state,
I turn my back to the window of opportunity.
The pain is too great.
Break the glass to deliver the metal,
strum the chords to my soul,
broken shards of myself have been left scattered
across the carpet floor,
fingers oozing my cries for silence,
trying to pick up the pieces,
drop by drop as the screams suffocate the cries from below.
There's a cold crisp stillness in the air as the flashing lights ask,
why so?

## 2.6. AH BON

Chirp,
swirl,
beam.
I lean,
there goes
my spleen.

A ray gleaming
through the frame,
same angle

I watch the weather change.
Beat blended with previous,
as I sigh,
"another day".

Body suspended in time

I lie & want to fade away.
Deaf tones made
as I scream
at the damned river.
Chained to my own slumber,
I cannot slither.

The swirling storm
of my mind dithers.

System down,
my yearning heart
withers.
Heal from this before I die?
Gasp,

I open my eyes.

I am just a
worthless liar,
pointless failure,
fickle self-loathing being,
waste of space.

Shed the scale of weight,
the cycle breaks.
A triumph today
is to levitate
from this linen grave.

Jump your lead
when the battery is down,
claw your way
to the surface,
do not drown.

Time to face what the world brings.
The alarm springs:

Ring,
ring,
ring.

## 2.7. THE DOOR TO A FRACTURED HOME

Tied to the hysteria of this area

stuck in limbo between guilt and living,

this flowering, peeling pain of once you wake

is the window to another lonely day.

We taste what it means to play their wicked game,

gluing our eyes to the blue, fluorescent light,

the beginning of the daily tunnel of self-hate,

glad to be away. Wish I stayed.

Sick to the stomach day-by-day.

I feel in flames.

## 2.8. MAS DRIPPING

As Sun Tzu,

O, master of war.

Addict to being slayed by thoughts,
a slave to my own grave.

Drowning,
from grape blood,

under razor blades
coming from the head
of a Moon hung in a cubicle.

Infused skin to tiles.

Lids heavy,

dead weight
heavier.

A carcass with a beating heart.

Awoken on the seabed
of the 4x4 ocean.

Trying to wash away the memory of the gale winds
that took you over the valley.

To slow the blitz
of panic,
I stampede over the same
bricks hoping something would change.

But my chest still burns,
I still whisper my wishes to the floor.

## 2.9. QUESTION MARK (?)

Have I lost a side that I held so dear inside?

The laughter, firecracker banter,

wasn't this supposed to make me feel more alive?

Dead end, if this doesn't work,

what's to say I just wasn't made for this?

The scary thing is,

now I've taken care of business

there are no more excuses.

I've done the work, so why do I still feel like this?

## 2.10. A ROSE GARDEN WITHOUT THE PETALS

Swaying like a cold summer breeze

Yet it's no breeze,

No breeze that's pulling up these trees

It's a "can't" storm

Shaking at the branches

Branching out for any type of vine-line

Droplets falling off the leaves drop by drop

Leaving me to drop to the canopy

Like the bird wrapped around my hand,

This is the pill to swallow,

My roots spreading keeping me at base

Product of my environment

Forest of blame and hate

A rose garden without the petals

The calm after the storm has settled

Dead leaves us all,

Confused, dazed, mazed, all in, but no idea where to go.

## 2.11. CULTURED NOOSE

I'm from the warm Mediterranean Sea
where the sand meets the shells
and the fish bombs, as we rebel.

I'm from an abusive lover
where, the salty skin of our existence
has been left out to dry,

by the night sky that's littered with
shards of the glass ceiling
and the stench of sewage,

attending mass, daily behind bars
of doodoo shots, whiskey on
the rocks, & speed bumps

has become a militant coping mechanism
for a population that prioritises
what's on the outside.

Lives left hanging by a foot,
electricity lines used in
a tug of war between militias.

I'm from a city that can't grasp
what a good night's sleep
will do to your health.

But who cares about our insides?
Politicians cough lies
line our horizon

of a better life in smog.
While we sit there unknowingly
waiting for our pulse to be flatlined.

Pitted craters between brother and sister.
Surely our souls and soles
are sore of fighting.

Why haven't we moved on from
what our ancestors didn't survive?
Our opportunities funnelled.
Our progress bottlenecked,
filtered to be stepped on
and decanted.

The most service we get
is the excessive honking on a stretch.
A daily reminder of our greatest strength
and biggest weakness everywhere we look.

I come from a country
where the seed of ana[2] can taste so bitter.
Where even our white flannels
have been ripped off of our humped backs.
Slums stacked,
white lies smacked,
left on our own two feet
with nothing but a flat arch.

The stink shrinks when the
pink clouds hide

the lack of peace,
the constant fight of the night sky,
while the
Church chimes
and the Mosque rhymes
clucking to the beat that we must
rise to our feet.



[2] Ana is an Arabic word that means 'me'.

CHAPTER 3

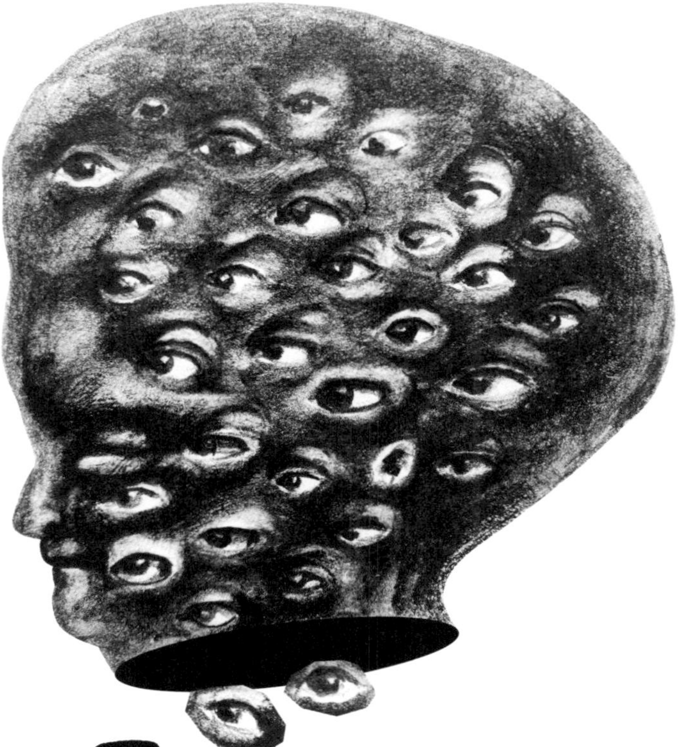

# TOAST TO MIDNIGHT: WORDS OF ABUSE

## 3.1. BOARDING A TRAIN

Zip-tied to lies we're
force fed in our adolescents.

Acronyms accredited like
dates during Ramadan.

Hinged to a leash of:
Disordered
Abnormal
Trouble enforcer.

Sin cos tan.

My biggest sin was
cause I couldn't tangibly
relate to their idea of success.

Of the system's diluted
message of importance.

The head cloning infants
on a conveyor belt of,
"Do your top button up".

Fucking stuck ups.

My brain chemistry
meant my mind's
geography was
way past the gates.

Displaced from the
tiny speck in the sea
"Yeah, you know Cyprus?
Syria?
Falasteen?

mmmm,
between the three".

*Bun the ruler*

A recital of my
personal bible.

Whilst everyone sang hymns,
almost tribal.

I just wanted to fly
high above the norm
didn't want to be like everyone
in the porn-infested dorms.

And it happened.
The penny dropped.

Between the second lesson
and the 4th teaching I handed out
in a bout on the 360.

I sussed it.
I cracked the code.

You see.

I was good at kicking the piggy,
okay at trigonometry,
but I was fucking good
at being fucking bad.

I finally got the attention
I thought I never had.

So,
whilst not caring about
what happened in '45,
or who you were or
how much your parents thrived,
I would just skive.

Why?

The monitor inside
created a thriving environment
for dreams of a clown.

Convinced that I was
saving his life by going down...
to the smoking trenches.

Drenched in questions,
wrestling my own Nazis
as children called me Islamy
and I donned a haircut
that'd best suit a Chad

or a Bradley.

All to fit in.

I started blazing to a level
just to pass,
not your common entrance
as I took a level of acting out.

To hiding in a bush of plant fertiliser
pushing 140 to match my heart's desire.
In for the kill of my innocence.
Benga, Coki, Mala as I skream,
SKREAMMMMM!!!!!!

## 3.2. LEFT FOOT RIGHT FOOT

As if,
a newborn
appeared in fall.

The baby
didn't know
how to stand
on their own,
two marshmallow
stilts.

Wheeled to the crowded
waiting room.
Awaited them
was a neigh-th of tranquilizer
and Gordon's.

Accompanied
this wake of the week.

The great
Devil's dandruff,
never a flake,
never asleep.

Normally
a treaty
to not sleep and
find it hard to have a stiffy,
paired
with greedy
pleads,

Please!
G,
I promise I'll rack up the next three!

Between me,
myself and lies.

This is the last time,
as the internal kettle has blown its top.

Railing the escape while fiends
over my shoulder waiting to take.

All, while
chasing that fleeting feeling

Of the rush
after the first brush
of the tusked
necklace, I ingest.

The phenomenon
of on the run
from one's emotions.
I'm addicted
to this commotion.

## 3.3. THE BIG SMOKE GOES 'POOF'

I left my pores on a dreary London City floor
mind,
          body,
                    & soul
nailed to an inch.

Soiled myself thinking I wasn't.
Sold my conscience to the
drip
         drip.

Jack, the lad,
picked up another packet.

Smile doesn't
tell you what an eye does.

Stay in line with bad habits
is the challenge.

One,     two,     drags

reminding you
that you're alive cuz,

I don't dance no more,
I don't need ya.

Feelings for where your urethra
should be, ugh.

Gotten to the stage
where it feels like it's beneath us.

Every day is a struggle
to keep my lips sealed.

Soppy fields with knockoff thrills
has got me popping pills.

Pissing away what mum and dad built,
something... something....
Pass me the bill.

## 3.4. STUTTERED SPEECH

Words left quivering on the top shelf, dust has flooded the dune of exchanges that should have been shared. Erosion of the colossus megalith that kept our community standing, resembled the lost Göbekli Tepe. Your slave, I tried lifting the burden, even when my back was frozen. Ice picks form in place of gratitude from decades of selfless acts to your extended. Expected handouts accompany rings on the hand held. Beings descending under one lineage shouldn't have to decipher scriptures of affection. The sedimentary trauma will rock an entire being into cognitive delay. Yesterday crosses over into today, brow slanted as I imagine what tomorrow looks like after death. Tell them love them. If not now?

When...

## 3.5. AFTER PARTY

Being released by the pair of bars
Life falling by the wayside
Everything turning pear shaped
Every time I look left and right they collide.
Mind, I've been left to let bare my mind,
Might leave to allow things to turn alright
Can I cut myself free from the binds that I've tied?
Pull the dagger I've lodged deep inside,
Set up lodge in the confines of the walls,
Gates of my seething plight
A plight to fight myself,
No more, I quiver with fright.
This burden is confusion.
Chaos seems like the only thing I know.

CHAPTER 4

# BINDING THINGS: WORDS OF EXPLORING

## 4.1. JOHNNY'S PLACE #1

Lagging from soaring across the globe
I stumble upon Johnny's world.

A café situated on a lake.

This is where
I'm going to have
my first Mexican taste.

At Johnny's place.

I bed myself at a table
draped with a garish purple
dress, provocatively it's
wooden limb inviting me in.

My walking sticks
sore, eyes droopy.
Some might say
looking a tad moody.

I gesture to the giddy waiter
with my paper changer, drenched
in coconut water, lime, and spice.

Una café por favor

aha, I'm already getting the hang of this.
I thought.

With my broken Spanish
and the overzealous
waiter's Spanglish
we reached a tangent.

I just wanted the café au lait

tired eyes,
still not quite sure
where I've arrived.

I sat back and there
loomed a breath of fresh
cigarette stench
coffee drenched, air.

I let roar a sigh,
it's good to be on the other side.

## 4.2. JOHNNY'S PLACE #2

Pick-up trucks dump
their morning frustration
onto the cobbled streets.

Young niños latched
to the backbone
of family wagons.

Greeting
fresh off the boaters,
remote workers,
& local homeowners.

Johnny's place
seems to be
where foreigners flee
to come and feed.

Out of the blue
swoop two
blackbirds.

Just one thing on their mind
to beat,
to a J-shaped,
man-made,
goods-bearing,
paw-printed
tree,
to the poor pigeon's
seed, already
in its tiny beak.

## 4.3. JOHNNY'S PLACE #3

Scanning the watering hole,
I drop my Eve's apple
on a herd of
unsuspecting tourists.

You see,
minding my own business
isn't
any of my business.

I'm a hunter, gatherer,
linguistic forager.
My nose for being nosey
knows no bounds.

My ear
draws near
to the dull & profound.
Eagle-eyed,

wedged between
a stump
and trencher,
I've found my next victim.

For conversation, prey
is my favourite meal
and this one seems plump,
rump, ready for picking.

## 4.4. MY FAVOURITE CONVERSATION TO DATE, IN JOHNNY'S PLACE:

How old are you, really?
She looks eerily.

My greys tell my date!
But, yours, hide your age...

Look at the state of my mane

She states with a glum disgrace.

Its ash wave whispers
my burnt-out fixture

one's tenure of this
venture

might show that I'm
ten years wiser.

To my surprise,
he replies,

Your waves
tell your years

My bags under
my eyes

tell mine.

He smiles as he
takes a bite of his pie.

## 4.5. NAKED DUSTING BEFORE NOON

Earthy eyes that invite

connection

Whispering pearly-white

complexion

Not a reflection of the

raging excitement

she has for the grand beauty

and a smoothie of a

butchered coconut with a straw

accompanied

with a

flakey almond croissant.

She's a noble island with

a wandering optic for the finer,

paints the town brighter

with her glistening designer.

You'll have to protect your neck

either from her witty sense

or her playful jest.

But don't mess

with the baby's intense

need to ingest the best.

Only blade sharper

than what she utters

are the high bones

that crack a smile.

Amongst the sass

& the class,

she's down to throw it down

at a taco diner with a fiver.

To venture on a journey to

the reckless side.

## 4.6. IPHONE HOLSTERED COWBOYS

Click, clack,
clickity, clackity,
a horse smacks
the pebbled track.

While the sun beats
off my leathery back.
A carriage brimming
with young niñas,

frothing from the seams
with excitement.
As if you stirred the local
Coca Cola with the cane,

boasting sashes tied
at their waists, a party
awaits. Tucked away
in the middle of the
quaintest Mexican place.

Sandwiched between
brutalist buildings; smeared
with vibrant paste & a grand
Church that just might
be a tad too big for this space.

A fiesta!
Confetti sprinkled with
mariachi zinging just
lovers swaying, rattling,
dancing in a cabaret.
Little toddlers and stray doggos
wanting to join the fray.
I perch myself from a safe place
gazing at everything at a crazy pace.

Watching over like a teta[3]
from her window frame.
Something catches my gaze.

A new age,
cowboy comes out from the shade
lifts his Rays, stays, and scours the plane.
My heart skips down the pathway
when he trots my way,
he neighs as he places himself
in the same paddock.

We could share the space, if his legs
didn't split The Channel,
The Gulf between my mind
and his mane,
Like Los Angeles' overpopulated
crazy 6 lane highways.

He lifts his dusty bowl, perched on
the forehead's horizon,
his hand travels as if Neo's
swatting Smiths off his visor
he reaches for his pocket
and pulls out a silver locket,
flicks the switch,
and out pops a bitch stick.

He proceeds to ask me for a flame,
I light with a sense of shame as I pry,
that once where a gun took place
now an iPhone lays.



3 Teta is an Arabic word that means 'grandmother'.

## 4.7. THE PEA DILEMMA

Excuse me,
Sir.
E e e xcuse me,
Waiter?
        3afwan[4],
            M3alem[5] ?!

            Ya Maître[6]!!

Keefak[7] ?
Ça va[8] ?

There seems to be
something in my creamy
chickpea.

I don't intend to offend
but this chickpea blend
with olive zest
and a bed of bread
has an alien friend.

Now I know this mash
has caused conflict
in the past.

But this problem is real

you see, there's
an invader in my land.
I just want to defend
from this strand
you understand...?

Silence filters into the cauldron of confrontation

[4] 3afwan is an Arabic word that means 'excuse me'.
[5] M3alem is an Arabic word that means 'sir', usually used to call out for a waiter.
[6] Ya Maître is Arabic and French for 'hey waiter'.
[7] Keefak is an Arabic word that means 'how are you?'
[8] Ça va? is french for 'are you ok?'

Habibi[9],
"There's a hair in my Hummus!"
Now, a disclaimer long flowing curls
isn't one of my features.

The waiter replies with a snide
"What would you like me to do,
dude?"
"Send it back for you?"
"How do I know it's not one of your bands?"
A flop that could cost
thousands of Lebanese pounds
leaves the server only with a firm murmur.

"How do you intend I prove
this booboo isn't indeed you?"

"A spy with kind blue eyes would
be your guise?"

"Make fly with your lies!"

And as simply as that

we had to attack
around the settlement
of our alien friend.

The creamy chickpea blend.



[9] Habibi is an Arabic word that means 'my dear'.

## 4.8. LAST CENTRAL TO FOREST

Evil screeching of tube lines,

hustle & bustle of rap rhymes,

clearance on the horizon,

to a moment of silence, divine

bars spat with harmonies from beaks,

broken shackles from London City streets,

this is where I'm meant to be.

Roots uprooted in defense,

from the rotting "I need to be someone" stress

pause

breathe

deep.

## 4.9. INCUBATOR WITH A POSSIBILITY OF INFECTION

To let the sea in is to accept the mother,

her nature is to ask me to rise,

knock knock, as she barks.

Hoping to son a germinating plant.

But I'm paralyzed on the bed of trees,

please let me be.

CHAPTER 5

# WAVING WHITE: WORDS OF LOVE

## 5.1. IN THE DUST BOWL OF LOST SOULS

After jumping into a leafy pit
muddled with running away
and trying to find a place,
came a tap on the shoulder & a
"Where can I set myself alight?"
asked the fieriest piercing,
yet, kindest bright eyes.
With a thick German might
the mysterious woman skipped
passed hellos and talk that was small.

On hand with bottled courage
and flames dancing straight, passed
the mundane straight into
"Why are your eyes in pain?"
We made little waste
of the only man made
construct that humans made
that might have a place.
As if her sharp sword like cheek bones
penetrated the armour that I thought
I left to support my heart from ache.
I opened the pearly floodgates,
daggers, fleeing from speech,
the purging of souls came to fruit,
a sop of sour stories bounced off
to assure each other we were ripe...
A gush of stillness seeping
through the cracks of our
conversation, I lay my vessel
on a plate, barely beating,
another weapon at face,
value equipped, she made haste
for my epicentre as she soared past
four legged cushioned perches.
Embraced me as if we had the
same DNA in a lifetime far away.

## 5.2. THIS IS A LOVE POEM

Well, I think it is
I guess there's a fine line.

You're like
a water droplet slowly
falling on a Rizla
when you're trying to roll a bifta.

Like the time
you're really fiending
for a digestive biscuit
but your little sister        nicked it.

Close to the time
where the clock chimes 9
but you forgot it was bank holiday Monday
and you're already on the subway.

You're like,
the beautiful breeze
swooping pollen through the East
when you really suffer from allergies.

And you know,
that thingy that opens the tinny?

Yeah,        you're like that,
but when it breaks
before you can get a taste.

You're the perfect clapback!
Only you arrive to the rhyme
by the time you're showering
off all that grime.

You're the sensation
when your navigation
is thrown into a whirlpool
as you miss that last step.

The beautiful freedom
when you've finally left your cave
to only be thrown in disarray
that you've left your keys in the tray.

Now,
picture a hot summer's day,
you're four drinks away
and your mate by mistake hands you the special K!

Yeah...

Ahhh that cozy rosy
commotion when you've roasted
on your favourite jeans.

Oh, those sweet lullabies.
When you've finally admitted defeat,
two bags deep and you go coocoo
from the pigeons woowoo.

Hold on...

Maybe you're not quite
as lovely
as I once thought you might be.

## 5.3. STARING MATCH WITH A SEAGULL

The graceful soft hum of her landing
on the deck of my existence
coincides with the freedom of
loving myself for the first time.

Clichés have no place in poetry
so I won't say that it feels like I've
met this seagull before
on a distant shore.

But when her wings are spread,
returning from exploring
lonesome endeavours.

A prickly rock bed
sprouts all over my sandy skin,
when her feathers wrap
around my organism,
just like mycelium.

Under the cover of the sea
that once crushed my body's
soil to oil, an enemy feeding,
turns once a bleak existence

to a flowering purple & yellow lake
of hope. Bound to self growth,
this isn't a mind field of toxicity.

But an exploration of two souls
only nailed to this earth
by the never tamed
frame that holds them.

Language interchanged by firing
hyphae-ced signals just by
locking the brown &
blue portals.

No longer waiting for the big bang
to create space, we hold it,
between the sweet bread
& brushing our beaks.

Endless possibilities but a mind trick
where the path migrates this.
Only hope is for the net
of previous failed conquests

to allow ourselves to flow mindful
along the winding river we
label existence and meet
flights of resilience,

with a soft underbelly of vulnerability
fused with a surfing for adventure
of this great body of water.
Is this what it feels to feel?

## 5.4. YOU SAY YOU'RE TOO MUCH

I say I can't get enough.
You state I'm the only bearer
of your insanity.
I state you drive me crazy
every time I handle you.
You preach self-love
and finding true connection.
I preach you've found it, but love,
you're terrified of the affection.
You offer an idea that we're worlds apart
but meant for one another.
I offer you what's left and implore you,
let's explore the undiscovered together.
You bridge the idea of lust
and setting you free if need be.
I bridge in suspension waiting
to see if ever you fly back to me.

You know; maybe just maybe,
I'm the one that's crazy?

## 5.5. YOU'LL PROBABLY NEVER KNOW

Like swings swaying in limbo.

Seaweed on the ocean floor.

I lie in the pool of reflection,

pitted to the acrylic seashell shores,

where I elongate and pick

at an anemone of my floating self

great barrier to my breath.

There's an anchor that melts

every time you touch.

I see Orion's belt

only thing left

is for you to know,

this is how

I've always felt.

CHAPTER 6

## 6.1. IS IT A HAVEN IF IT'S NOT SAFE?

Succumbed to your
drip feeding of love,
I can't help but prance in
the wide fields of cotton buds.
That you've stitched upon
every promise you've ever
touched. Within the wild lust
you mutter to the gods.
Once ushered into a self
induced cocoon of a safe bosom.
Hidden away from day-to-day,
seemingly afraid to intertwine
minds with different tribes.
Interactions had become
fractured. Mastered the art
of draping the cover over face.
Now, a welcoming party awaits
at a house built to upstand
the traits I aim to wake.
Coupled with hope and grandeur,
a season has come to blossom
to relax that once suffering lip
& drop feed the decree
that I am to be set free.

## 6.2. MEDITATING ON A JIU JITSU MAT

Healings hit differently

when it's towards the back

that strike first on the sharp path

that rests

between the brambly bleeding

bushes signifying lineage.

Checkpoint reached as I

was asked to go right

with Charlie; what's left?

Long pause

Shy of eye

because I'm scared

they'll tell the truth,

the whole, not broken

but this poem,

isn't about the past,

it's about shedding

dull patterned layers.

Cracking between them,

waves of salty new

sails of,

if I only knew.

Index touches thumb

flicks off crumbs

from the sheets of numb.

I will allow myself

to feel

what's to come.

Juice of a blood moon

seeping through,

dew of confidence

waning true,

my new cycle

is due.

## 6.3. ORAL RUTTIER TO A PANOPTIC GARDEN

Unsettled sail findings

As the horizon merges the sky with the sea,
marrying two grand forces.
They dissolve into one colour
of the deepest blue,
akin to the depth of sorrow connected to loss.

Look down below you,
towards your writing hand.
There resides
a circular pool of fluorescent green,
bright as a meadow in full season.

Sail a length of your boat,
bear left and go.
Go forwards with the crisp wind,
a wind flying along the lines of biting
into a lightly seasoned potato
fresh out of the fire with garlic and rosemary.

That taste won't bear fruit
for more than a few shrieks
of the trailing gulls.
Whilst they're circling your vessel praying
for any scraps to jump ship.

You'll taste the air change,
the heat will dissolve to sweat.
A marriage of a sense of jasmine,
a dash of olive with a sprinkle of sea salt.

Let the taste become thicker

and your flickering eye will catch
an eggshell shaded crack breaking the coupling.
Arched with great waves it rests atop
a bed of beads and pebbles. Not clear
to the naked eye what's between the four walls.

Let your mind decide what lies inside
but beware before you enter.
There's a slippery green
moss
awaiting you at the shore.

## 6.4. THE MONTH OF DECEMBER

When the clouds start to descend on us,
tremble us with their tremendous;

torturous,
treacherous
living spectacles of us.

Inequitable showers coming from
the mountains that tear us apart,

debatable actions caused
by the reactions of our gods,

spitting bolts to cause

our thunder to muster

every single one to take part.

this is a rallying cry,

to spend the nights alive,
bounded by bandages
with brothers and sisters
with a vision in sight.

The chains
that shackled us to the ground,
bestowed upon us by the ruling,

have shapeshifted to a bond between

man

making us be on our toes and fight.

A tip with flare,
    we dare to kick
back their tear gas,

with a volley in our red mist.
we are not alone.

They come in numbers
with obvious muster
to stand in our way.

We are not afraid!

Rocks flying
opening our eyes
to what side you try.

Try as you might.

We will not bite
to this genocide
of our rights.

## 6.5. IN THE WING OF A MIRROR

Birds singing the Spring greeting.
Beams seeming to peer through to say hello to you.
Flowers blooming, trees blossoming, fields alight with life.
It smells like rebirth is rife in plain sight.

–

Yet, I miss the shots of rifles in the sky.
Slammers pounded against the brass tax in remembrance of our last.
The hustling, bustling, busting out of each corner crevasse.
Dodging the teething beings in their iron deathtraps doing laps to make an end.
Electronic strings swing from building to building to keep the illusion of being a thing.
Made up thugs in their iron hubs pushing us apart.
In a time of flowing, growing, and showing myself on a mast,
I can't help but to look over my shoulder and not miss the past.
An organism that just doesn't have a beginning or an end.
A cycle of repetitive beats that is hanging on by the skin of its teeth.
Family, friends, brothers, sisters, I sign off with a droplet of trust,
that our future will thrust us to be together again.
Whatever needs must.
We will be home.
Home.
Never alone.

## 6.6. OWLS FLY IN SILENCE

What muffled the fluttering joy of my hood you ask?
The child within has begun to waver thin.
No more wide smile my dear.
Chin to chin has become sin to sin.
An acorn should germinate into a tree
but my germs are infected.
I struggle to dig deep and plant my seed,
oh, how I look for a profound sense of being.
Turning the pages to find my why.
Dry tears gather mass inside.

My oh my, can I cry.
While I attempt to comprehend
to why I don't prevail,
I keep proceeding for this needing feeling.
Resentment is smeared like the scent of rotting roadkill.

Pause, as I inhale,
and smell the stench
I
        spit.
                Treating the beating;

Keeping.
Fleeting.
Wheeling.
Pealing.

## 6.7. DRIP DRY

Sobering thoughts
25th of October
to now what?

3 months
14 weeks
98 days
2,342 hours
104,551 minutes

And the seconds,
they keep on changing.

My mind,
the same thing.

Manage big deals
with bigger hangovers.

Attributing my personality
with fat keys of vanity.

The tragedy.

I couldn't see
the damage,

backbone fixed
with a tranquilliser fix,
weekly ticks of
getting the social kick.

As I consume booze
to make you and your
best Icarus impression
digestible.

COME AGAIN MY SELECTA!!!

With arms flailing
gun fingers waving
& screams in the Middle East,
of London
YALLA[10]
accompanied.

A mark with a hook and a dot under,
lumber to the juncture that the answer
won't be found on a white porcelain beach
littered with straws & 10-pound sheets.
But the loudest bitch is the internal pitch
rattling from the bomb-boxed sphere.

Clawing it to disappear.



[10] Yalla is an Arabic word that means 'quickly'.

## 6.8. HACK-NEY WEEDS

Sabotage

is a dish best served

when the garden is flourishing.

The infestation of,

"I don't deserve"

finds a home within my psyche.

I watch it

coil around my bark,

asphyxiating the trunk of gratitude,

satellites

of intrusive murmurs creating

a blanket of dew

filled with gloom.

Fog rolling punches

incessantly

plowing at the soil of a clear thought.

Leaves an indigenous forest

seeded with the rape of,

"you've grown so much".

A monoculture of a singular crop

that tastes of,

"I'm not good enough",

sprouts randomly,

on a walk,                on the bus,

when I'm picking Uma's muck.

The pitchfork in the trail of,

"Will I let this be my last stock,

or can I spring into life once more?"

is held up by the scarecrow that only

frightens themselves with the twisted

hay bales as brains.                Whilst

parasites lay wait.

Mental nutrients

drained, the need for clippings to be

cut to create a clearing.

A new season

approaches, this harvest

just won't feed,                I think,

it's time to plant a new tree.